Keisha's Wondrous Christmas

By Carolyn Sahaja Willis

This is a work of fantasy fiction centered on a real life companion, Keisha. I have hopes that she experienced everything that spoke to my imagination.

SUMMARY: Keisha has an unexpected encounter with Mitzi, a wild rabbit. Keisha will learn an important lesson while helping restore a home and making new friends. Mitzi has many fairy friends. Together, they have a special Christmas celebration.

Cover design and interior photography by Carolyn Willis

Back cover photograph by Carolyn Bezona

Dedicated to all Service Animals everywhere.

ACKNOWLEDGEMENT

I thank the members of the Lakebay Writers, Key Center, Washington who provided supportive criticism for my weekly readings of the developing chapters.

.

Table of Contents

1. Carolyn's Gift to Keisha

Morning chore time at Seud Araidh, Carolyn and her four-legged furry friends' little five acre estate, was taking a bit more time than usual. Keisha was eager for her doggie cookie. She always got one, but only after her outside friends were fed.

"Ruff. Arff, arff," Keisha barked which meant: Hurry, hurry, hurry. I need my cookie.

Keisha soon realized something was different. She thought Carolyn might be a bit confused this morning. *Why is she closing gates that are usually left open and opening gates that are always closed?*

This unusual activity started as soon as pony, Shugyr, came in from the back woods and into the front pasture. Carolyn closed the woodland gate. Shugyr would not be able to return to the woods after breakfast. Now she was sharing the same pasture as llama, El Duende, and the angora goats, Kindle and Hanna.

Keisha watched a most peculiar thing happen next. Carolyn opened all the backyard gates and walked away.

"Woof, woof, gerr woof. Look, look, here."

Keisha was trying to point out the mistake, running back and forth between the open gates and Carolyn.

Carolyn understood the excited running around and barking. "It's okay Keisha." Carolyn bent down and petted her beloved dog's head, Keisha's second favorite spot.

"It is for you, sweetheart."

Keisha was very confused, but soon learned, while getting her favorite tummy rub, that it was no mistake.

"I'm leaving the backyard open to the woods as a special Christmas present for you. Duende, Shugyr, and the goats will have to make do with the front pastures for Christmas Eve. You can go into the woods and have fun."

Keisha enjoyed the freedom to explore the woods, all the holes and thicket paths, and especially all the smells left by the other inhabitants. She could not do it often, and it was very tempting. Yet, she never liked leaving her friend, even when Carolyn told her to go play.

But . . . this is a Christmas present. Carolyn will be alright, for a little while without me, she assured herself as she looked to the woods and back to Carolyn.

"Go play, Keisha." Carolyn continued to encourage her dog to have some fun.

Keisha was a very loyal companion and it was difficult for her to leave.

Carolyn kneeled on the ground, ruffled Keisha's fur, and then pulled a doggie cookie from her pocket.

"Here. You don't even have to come in the house for your cookie."

After her customary quick-sniff inspection, Keisha gently took her favorite snack, lay down, and in less than a blink, chewed it up and swallowed.

Yum. I love cookies. She looked at Carolyn who always had to show that her hands were empty.

"All gone, darling. Now, go play. Shoo, shoo." Carolyn waved her hands. "Go play!"

Keisha's adventuresome spirit got the best of her. She thought, *it will be fun. It is a wonderful Christmas present.* "Ruff ger ruff ruff er-roff. I will leave for just a little while."

4

2. The Unexpected Encounter

Keisha trotted off down the trail, her nose to the ground checking out all the different smells. Carolyn turned back to the house, smiling at the thought of her dog playing in the woods.

Keisha loved one special little woodland place in Seud Araidh. Carolyn calls it the Fairy Glen. Why, I wonder? That's where I'll go play.

Neither Keisha nor Carolyn had ever seen any fairies. It was, however, a nice thought that mystical little beings might live in this quiet woodland. It had a mysterious silence about it. Outside sounds seemed far distant whenever she and

Carolyn sat in the glen's center on a garden bench she had placed just off the trail. She often told Keisha they should watch for the possibility of seeing fairies.

"Ya never know," Carolyn would say and wink.

On this day, Keisha wasn't going to look for fairies. *Too many wonderful smells to investigate. I'll leave the fairy watching to her. This is my Christmas present.* Her nose twitched with anticipation and she sniffed the air.

A beautiful, tree-lined path meandered to the fir-bordered circle at the center of the one acre glen. Sunbeams trickled through the trees casting ever changing shadows along the way. Keisha took some time to get to the center, even though the entire length of the trail was less than a hundred feet.

There was much to explore. Little holes some creature had burrowed through the moss next to an exposed fir root. A little thicket-roofed path leading into a small marsh. And a tall stack of limbs Carolyn had piled up after a wind storm.

Keisha knew Carolyn meant to chip these limbs, then scatter them on the path, but the stack had been there for two years. Time enough had passed for tiny creatures to consider it permanent. Many had made the mound their home above, within, and below.

Today, Keisha discovered a small, freshly dug hole at the mound's edge. Because she loved to dig, further investigation was irresistible. She pushed her nose down into the soft black dirt and began biting out large chunks of moss until a salal root obstructed her progress. She used her front paws to enlarge the hole and her teeth to tug on the root.

She was a skillful digger and took great pride in making big holes in the earth. She progressed quite nicely and was having fun making dirt fly as she dug faster.

The noise attracted the inhabitants of the glen who became worried when they saw how deep the dog had dug into the mound of limbs. Now only her fuzzy, short, wagging tail was visible from under the mound's edge.

Keisha was focused on her digging. *What a wonderful day. Thank you Carolyn. I will check on you right after I pull out this root.*

6

She tugged with all her might, jaws clamped tightly around the root, dirt and all—growling continuously. Tug. Tug. Puuullllll. "Geeerrrr. Let loose you stubborn root."

She pushed hard with her back legs, now tucked under her belly, hoping this would help pull out the root. The root didn't move, but her attempts to pull it out caused small limbs and dirt to fall from the surface of the mound and land on her exposed rump.

"Get out of here you nasty dog! Shoo! Shoo! Squeal, squeak. And fill the hole back in as you leave. You are letting in all the cold air. Squeeeeak eeeeeek squeeeealllll." A very insulting rabbit who had an ear piercing scream advanced toward her in a most hostile manner, while baring its teeth.

"Wow. Woof errr ouf? Yikes. What is that doing here?"

Surprised by this rabbit's aggression, Keisha growled. The root slipped so quickly out of her mouth that she plopped onto her stomach with a thud. She was very embarrassed. Now she needed to defend her dignity as well her right to dig wherever she pleased.

Keisha never took kindly to being told she couldn't burrow anywhere she pleased—like the time she dug up all the dahlia bulbs. The earth had been tilled and was soft and perfect for a delightful dig. Her friend Carolyn was as displeased then as this bossy rabbit was now.

Well, she had learned not to dig in areas Carolyn called the garden, but this was different. "How dare you tell me I cannot dig in my own glen."

"Out. Out, I say. Eee. Eee. Screeeech." The little brown rabbit jumped fearlessly toward this canine intruder who was nearly four times bigger, and nipped it smartly on its nose.

"Ouch. Yip. That hurt! Errrr." Keisha bumped her head on the low ceiling and some dirt fell on her face. This only made her angrier. "Get out of my way you bad rabbit. I want to dig. Gerrrrrr woooof."

If humans had been standing close by, they would have only heard yips, squeals, squeaks, growls, and muffled barks. However, out of all this doggy and rabbit chatter some may have recognized an actual squabble between two very determined critters.

"Squeeeek eeee. You are making the tunnel much, much too large. Coyotes could now crawl into my beautiful den. I had it all safe and cozy for winter. You're biting and clawing is tearing it apart. Out I say!"

The rabbit leaped forward and nipped Keisha's nose again. Then she quickly turned around and thumped the dog's face repeatedly with her powerful back legs, throwing paws-full of dirt in Keisha's face.

Keisha was already struggling to back out. "I was just exploring. Don't get so bothered. It's not such a big hole. I have barely enough room. Aaaachoooo!" The dirt in her nose made her sneeze.

"But look at me you oversized-red-fur-ball. I'm a quarter your size. And the raccoons are half your size and. . . . Oh my-eeee, they are such a tremendous bother." The rabbit began thumping Keisha again.

"Now those lazy good-for-nothings will be able to push into my little den, and I will have to find a new home. It's winter you know." She gave the dog two final good wallops. Thump, thump.

"Ouch! Ouch! Arf! Arf!" Keisha didn't see the rabbit wallops coming. She had been struggling to back out and was bewildered by the rabbit calling her an 'oversized-red-fur-ball.'

"Oh! Whatever will I do?" The little rabbit was not really talking to Keisha any longer. She started hopping back and forth between her crumbling burrow and tunnel entrance, screaming and squealing.

To make matters far worse than the destruction from digging, every move that Keisha made trying to back out caused everything to crumble even more.

The rabbit instinctively removed a bit of earth from one fur-lined corner, and continued to mumble her grievances as even more bits of earth rained down on her and into her home. "Everything was ready for Christmas. My family is coming over from Huckleberry Field, and we were going to have a delightful dinner in my new den."

She didn't stop voicing her dismay as a plop of earth fell on her fuzzy, brown head. The dirt clump rolled over her right ear causing it to flop down. Then the clump fell to the ground.

Keisha finally took notice of how distressed the little creature was. "Can't you just fill it in? After all, it only took me seconds to dig through here."

The furious little rabbit turned toward the dog. "You collapsed half of my roof, you dweeb! My nice covering of branches is now falling into my tunnel. What am I to do about that?"

While pointing to several limb ends slipping into the tunnel, the troubled rabbit's scolding turned into a mournful moan. "This is hopeless." Still, she continued to pick up branches. The task seemed impossible to the little rabbit. "But, I can't abandon my dream."

The dog watched the rabbit struggling to save her home. Now, Keisha was not at all fond of rabbits. "Annoying little creatures," she always grumbled, "who never asked permission to hop all over my yard whenever they pleased."

However, Keisha was beginning to feel guilty after realizing she had destroyed someone's home. Tears streamed down her fuzzy face as she remembered past sadness in her life when years ago Carolyn rescued her from a frightening building. Keisha remembered losing her first home and feeling alone in a cement-floored pen surrounded by strangers: uniformed people, barking dogs, and howling cats. Since that day, when Carolyn lifted her onto the front seat of the car, her only worries became small things like having to share pillows and space on the bed with Mischief Kitty.

"I'm sorry little rabbit. I will leave you alone." Keisha had only her front shoulders and head to pull from the tunnel.

"You're, sorry. That's it? You're sorry?" Large clumps of the roof were dropping on their heads.

While hopping over the dog's face to scramble from the collapsing den and tunnel, the rabbit continued complaining. "It took me all summer to make my wonderful home. You've ruined it, don't you see?"

As Keisha's head popped from the hole, she turned around and saw the rabbit glaring at her. "Can't you just build a new one?" Keisha asked. "It seems a simple thing to do." Keisha shook her body all over to get rid of the dirt clinging to her coat. It was making her itch so she also scratched behind her ear with a rear paw.

The rabbit tried to duck from this new rain of dirt clumps that flew from the dog. "Just build a new one? Simple? How rude." The rabbit complained to herself, ignoring the dog. She hopped around the pile of limbs that had protected her den. The damage caused her so much distress, her mumblings suddenly became a piercing squeal of anger.

"That dog trashes my burrow, and then tells me to 'just build a new one.' I had it just the way I liked it." The rabbit cried, "My new home—gone." The last despairing word squeaked out as a hopeless whimper, muffled further because her head had nodded down into her furry chest.

The rabbit took a moment to look at the mess before continuing her lament. "I am going to have to ask my family if I can live with them for the winter until I find a new place. It was crowded there and oh, so peaceful here living with my new friends.

"That's it, I'll ask them if they can help me. Oh! This is terrible. Oh, I can't ask them because they are so tiny. They can't lift this mess or dig a new tunnel. Well, maybe I could live with them for a little while. Oh, I really don't know what to do."

The rabbit was talking so fast Keisha could barely understand everything, but the rabbit caused her to wonder who else lived in her glen. *What tiny friends is that rabbit talking about? I don't see anyone.*

All at once the rabbit stopped her lament, looked up and saw Keisha was still there—just standing and staring at her. She twitched her nose to show her contempt.

"Well, silly dog. Are you going to just stand there all day, or are you going to help me? We rabbits are very determined critters, and this rabbit is no exception."

"Help you? I don't know what to do." In truth, Keisha was totally amazed by the request.

"Help me repair my home, you twit. You can dig and pick up limbs. You can restore the branches over my burrow, and repair the tunnel while I clean out my den." In spite of everything that just happened, she had not quite given up on rebuilding her crumbling home. She was willing to recruit anyone, even this horrible dog.

"I dig holes. I am a master digger. I don't build tunnels, and I don't know how to repair the mound of branches. That is not what I do!"

Keisha was quite put out that this silly rabbit was commanding her to do things. She was not a builder, and she was going to make that perfectly clear. "I am a digger and a 'pull-a-part-er' and good at it! Ask those friends you were talking about to help you. I don't know how to build a roof of limbs. I pull limbs out of piles, not into them."

And that is that, Keisha affirmed to herself as she sat down and licked her paw, acting nonchalant.

The rabbit was not listening to Keisha's defense. She was trying to clean up a giant cave-in using her front paws to dig back into the den while her hind legs kicked out the dirt. Scratch! Scratch! Thump! Thump!

Keisha's dog-driven curiosity caused her to get a bit too close. She kneeled on her forepaws with her rump high in the air, creeping into the tunnel to watch just as the rabbit kicked out some dirt.

Whap! The dirt landed squarely on Keisha's face. "Hey rabbit! Watch what you're doing."

The rabbit turned to see the dog with a plop of dirt on its nose and its red facial hairs dusted earth brown. She couldn't help but smile at the sight of the silly-looking dog. Her smile quickly faded and became a frown with her ears downcast.

Keisha destroyed yet another section of the mound as she scrambled free of the flying dirt.

Shaking her head and sneezing, she then plopped on her side to rub her body and head on the moss-covered forest floor. All the while, as she cleaned herself, she complained, concluding her grumblings with, "Stupid rabbit."

3. One by One, by Every One

"Oh, my. Oh my. Now look what you have done." The rabbit was sitting on her haunches in front of her completely collapsed doorway. Overcome with the disaster, the poor rabbit could not even squeal. Her little world was in turmoil. She began to cry, silently at first, and then it became a rabbit stuttering sniffle. Tears flowed from her brown eyes onto her little fuzzy cheeks, then dropped to the freshly fallen earth that had been her tunnel roof.

Keisha rolled from her side onto her stomach. Her red-freckled, white paws were almost touching the sad rabbit.

Carolyn cried sometimes, which made Keisha feel helpless. It was very confusing not knowing how to help. *No,* she thought to herself, *crying is a bad thing.*

Seeing the rabbit cry made Keisha feel very sad. "Don't cry rabbit. It's okay."

The rabbit fell to her side, hiccupping between panting. "My—my naa—ame is na—na not Ra—bi—bit. My—my name is Mitzie. And it is na—not, okay. I have no—no place to sleep to-'*hic*'- night that is—is safe. The raaa—coons can get in, and if it- '*hic*'- rains or snows, I will be, be verr—ry cold. I will haf—have to live with my parents again, '*hic*' and it is verr—ry crowded. I so wanted, '*hic*,' my own place, and it was so beautiful, '*hic*.'"

"I'm sorry rabbit, ah, Mitzie. I didn't mean to do anything wrong. I was just digging and having fun. I didn't realize I was destroying someone's home."

Keisha laid down on her stomach. Now, both animals were crying face to face. A little pond of tears formed and wet the ground beneath their muzzles.

"I have never built anything. I only know how to pull things out. Maybe you can teach me. I will try very hard. My Carolyn always says I'm a very smart doggess. I'm sure I can learn to put sticks back in a pile.

"I remember watching Carolyn drag limbs and pile them up, one at a time. I'll do that."

Mitzie was still sniffling, but the tears and hiccups stopped. "You will help me?"

"I promise I will try. My name is Keisha. What do we do first?" Keisha, ready to help, jumped to her feet, which of course would have startled any rabbit.

Mitzie tried to run, but had barely enough energy to jump back one little step. Staring at the dog, she thought: This is amazing. This dog just offered to help me rebuild my burrow, but what do I tell it to do first? I have never talked to a dog, let alone teach one to build a burrow . . . and, can I trust it?

Mitzie struggled to speak. "I'm not really sure. The entrance is all dug up, and the hole that is left is way too big. Maybe, if you could fill in the old tunnel, I might be able to find a good place to dig a new one . . . and the limb pile needs to be re-stacked."

14

Mitzie pointed to the branches that were scattered hither-and-yon around the mound. She picked up one of the smallest twigs in her mouth, and hopped to an edge of the tilting brush pile. She stood as tall as possible, and dropped the twig neatly on top of another limb. Then she pulled one of the displaced branches, trying to straighten the arrangement.

Keisha copied what Mitzie did, picking up a larger limb at its middle to balance the weight. It was the first one she pulled off the pile earlier, which caused smaller ones to fall to the ground. She carefully climbed up some limbs, placed her branch on top of the pile, backed down, and went for another.

"Maybe this won't be so hard," she mumbled as she clamped her jaws around a second branch.

Amazed, Mitzie's little jaw dropped. "Very nice. Can you continue replacing and arranging the limbs as I dig a new tunnel on the backside?"

"Yes. I think I can do that."

Keisha began to work. One by one, by every one, she did her best to put the limbs back exactly where they had been. The branches that fell into the den had to be pulled out from the top and re-stacked.

She thought as she worked. This building is a strange concept. Totally not one of my usual doggess routines. I don't even like to play fetch. Carolyn soon learned this, and now plays my favorite game—Keep-A-Way. She visualized Carolyn finding a nice stick and pretending to reach for it.

I grab it first, and then Carolyn tries to get it back.

Sometimes Carolyn just sits or rolls on the ground while trying to reach for my stick. Running circles around her is fun, too.

Keisha smiled with a limb in her mouth thinking. It's a grand game, and it always ends with a little wrestling, and a lot of hugs, and pets, and tummy rubs.

Carolyn would delight in watching me learn how to place sticks and branches in their proper places. Well, I hope I'm doing it right. These branches will help protect the rabbit's burrow.

As Keisha was stacking limbs, she watched Mitzie kicking dirt into the old entrance, then pounding it firmly with her back legs. Keisha helped finish filling in the hole and put branches over the fresh dirt. Mitzie hopped to the other side of the limb mound to finish the new tunnel.

Time passed in quiet, thought-filled labor. *How long have I been here? Maybe hours.* Keisha hurried to finish, covering the old tunnel entrance with more branches. *Carolyn will be checking on me. I need to go home.*

Sure enough, not long after that thought, Carolyn called, "Keisha, come. Come girl. Where are you? Keisha, come."

4. There You Are

Keisha always went to Carolyn when she called. "I'm sorry Mitzie. I have to go home for a while. Carolyn is calling me. I'm almost finished stacking the limbs, and you have finished the tunnel. I will try and come back later." Keisha trotted towards home leaving Mitzie to scoop out her den.

Mitzie was grateful for the help, but, instead of saying thank you, she mumbled to herself, "Yeah, right. I'll never see you again."

Carolyn was still calling her favorite 'doggess' just as Keisha got to the trailhead.

"There you are my darling. Having some fun in the Fairy Glen, I see. I'm so glad. I wanted you to play. And . . . from the look of your dirty face you did. Just look at you.

"I peeked at you throughout the day. You were having lots of fun pulling on sticks and digging. Must be something really interesting in that old mound of limbs. I had lots of things to do too, so I didn't bother you. But, I missed you."

Carolyn affectionately brushed off Keisha's dusty head. "Good dog. Champion digger.

"Hey. How did you get those two nicks on your nose?" Carolyn knelt down for a closer inspection. Keisha tried to duck away, but Carolyn was holding her muzzle.

"Curious. You must have cut your nose on a sharp stick. They are small cuts though. You'll be fine." Carolyn ruffled Keisha's neck again then kissed the top of her head between her ears.

Keisha turned quickly away to avoid the subject. "Arf woof woof. Let's go feed my friends," Keisha barked as she trotted off to the front pasture. *I have so much to tell them.*

Carolyn recognized her dog's behavior. "You want to feed the critters? Well, okay. Let's get it done. It is just an hour early, and I'm sure they think they're starving."

"Whinny." One perpetually starving, fat pony agreed with her loud neigh and several head nods.

"Hummmm. I'm hungry too," said the llama, El Duende.

"Baa. Us too," blatted the goats, Hanna and Kindle.

Keisha jumped happily about as she followed Carolyn. "Woof, gurrr-woof woof. Yeah. Feed the critters. I need to tell them about Mitze."

While Carolyn was getting the critter's feed, Keisha rushed to her friends and shared what had happened in the fairy glen. Shugyr, El Duende, Hanna and Kindle eagerly listened to the whole adventure.

"So I am going back in a little while to help Mitze finish repairing the damage."

Just then, Carolyn came around the barn carrying two squares of hay and three cans of grain. She stopped when she saw Keisha standing close to the fence barking non-stop at the pony, llama, and goats. "Well, that's unusual."

The pony and llama were leaning over the fence with their noses almost touching Keisha. The goats were poking their noses through the fence wire.

Carolyn shouted, "Hey you guys. What's going on? You critters seem to be having a conversation."

Keisha immediately stopped barking and the critters quickly backed away from the fence.

Shugyr whinnied to Keisha. "Be sure to come back in the morning to tell us what happened."

Carolyn opened the barn door and began distributing the feed including some treats of apples and carrots.

Usually the critters would rush in to eat, but they were taking their time, stopping occasionally to whinny, blat, and hum while looking directly at Keisha who seemed to be barking a response.

Carolyn was very curious. *How strange.* "I wish I could understand what you all are saying to each other this evening. You have never done this before. As far as I know anyway. Maybe it's a Christmas Eve thing. Is that it, Keisha?"

Keisha looked directly at Carolyn and her tongue began a high-pitched, trilling doggie laugh which Carolyn said sounded like a Zaghareet—a Middle Eastern greeting. "Laa-laa-laa-trill-trill-laa-laa-laa."

When Keisha stopped "laughing" she barked her answer, "Not exactly, but it is an exciting story." Only the animals understood.

Keisha now started running back and forth between the other animals barking non-stop. "Hurry up you guys. The very best part of this job is after Carolyn feeds you. I get a cookie. Love my cookies. Woof! Yip yip! Yipppppeeeee! Hurrah!"

Shugyr stared at the dog and nickered. "Yes, we know. So you can stop telling us. You're very loud, you know."

"Woof. Sorry."

After everyone got their oats, hay, treats and fresh water, Keisha ran up the front stairs and into the house. Her cookies were kept in a gallon jar on the kitchen table. In the evening, first she got a cookie, and then Carolyn gave her some crunchy dog chow and checked the water bowl, and fed Mischief her tuna chow.

For herself, Carolyn made a simple dinner that didn't take longer than five minutes. Keisha knew cooking was not Carolyn's thing. A baked potato in the microwave with a bit of cheese and a cup of hot chocolate was a three course dinner. Keisha liked eating the potato skin, and of course, licking the plate.

Tonight was no exception. "Togetherness. Eh what Keisha darling?" Carolyn put the plate down on the floor. "What friends don't know, friends don't need to know."

Keisha didn't understand why friends would mind them sharing a dinner plate, so no comment was heard from her as she licked up the last of her potato entree.

It was nearing sunset before Carolyn nodded into an after dinner nap. Keisha didn't want to leave, but she had promised to help Mitzie finish the burrow. Squeezing through the opening Carolyn left in the sliding door for Mischief Kitty to get in and out, Keisha hurried to the woods.

5. Keeping a Promise

The air was frosty. A perfect Christmas Eve. Keisha found she was enjoying her evening trot on the glen path. Her ears perked forward listening to woodland sounds.

The setting sun must be sparkling off the wet leaves. Keisha watched lights dancing from tree to tree. Strange? I have never seen that before.

Stranger than that, as she approached the trail, she heard giggles. Then she was almost certain she heard someone speaking in a very sweet little voice.

"Hush everyone. Here she comes. Quiet."

The giggling silenced and the twinkling lights blinked out. The lights stirred Keisha's curiosity. But their suddenly going out scared her. Her body trembled.

Now the trail was shadowed in woodland darkness. Keisha imagined she felt the silhouettes of tree branches nibbling at her toes. The absence of the mysterious voices did not make her feel any better. Frightened, she hoped she was not alone.

"Mitzie, Mitzie. Are you here?" Keisha crept to the mound.

This is strange. Is it the shadows that make the place look so different? It looks like no cave-in occurred at all.

She put her nose close to the ground and sniffed. Everything seems carpeted with fresh, green moss scattered with crisp brown and golden winter leaves.

"Mitzie? Did you do all this? It looks great. Mitzie?"

Mitzie smiled, watching Keisha focused on the ground. How surprised she would be if she looked up. My friends are everywhere. Some are sitting on tree branches, and others are fluttering about. They all have their hands over their mouths, trying not to laugh.

Mitzie could barely keep from hopping out to tell Keisha everything. But, it was agreed that this was to be a surprise. While Keisha was gone, fairies had been helping Mitzie finish rebuilding her home.

Some had finished the limb pile. It took ten faries to lift one limb and place it on top of the mound. Others brought Mitzie some wool that had been dumped close by. Swarms of fairies had lifted the nicest tufts and flown through the tunnel entrance into the burrow. Each tuft of white llama, sheep, or angora wool was carefully felted onto all the walls, the ceiling, and the floor.

Mitzie and her friends couldn't suppress their giggles. *Yes*, Mitzie thought, *Keisha is going to be very surprised.*

"Mitzie? Are you here? Is that you giggling?" Keisha found the new tunnel entrance, and was very careful as she lowered her forepaws onto the forest floor. Her little stubby tail was unusually still.

Did Mitzie fix all this and still move to Huckleberry Field? She wondered while peering into the dark hole.

"Yes, Kiesha. I'm here."

Keisha had been hoping Mitzie would answer. Nevertheless, the interrupted silence startled her, and her rump collapsed to the ground.

"Elm Dust said to come on in," a voice said in the darkness.

Almost undetectable giggles floated throughout the glen. Keisha moved only her eyes, looking for who was laughing.

"Come in? Are you crazy? I'll break it all down again. Stop joking around. How did you get all this finished by yourself? And it's so beautiful. I can't even tell anything happened. It's better than . . . did you say elm dust?" Keisha raised her head to think better.

"What's elm dust?" *How can dust tell me to come in*? Then Keisha realized it could not be dust. "Did you say Elm Dust said to come on in? Good Grief. Not another rabbit." Keisha moaned.

Keisha lowered her head again to peer inside. The hole, smelling of freshly dug earth, was so enticing she had to force herself not to dig.

In the darkness, Mitzie was barely visible as she hopped closer to the entrance and Keisha. "Yes. Elm Dust is one of my friends who helped finish my burrow. We gathered some wool Carolyn had thrown away. I hope that is okay. Then we picked through the piles and found some really nice pieces. My entire burrow is now lined with wool. It is soooo cozy. Please say 'thank you' to your human."

Keisha's eyes squinted trying to focus on the hopping rabbit. "I will do my best, but she will probably not miss it at all. She said it was not good for spinning into yarn. Carolyn said she hoped some small critters could use it, but she worried it would not be good enough for anything."

"Oh most of it worked quite nicely. Come in. See for yourself."

"Mitzie. You know I won't fit through the tunnel."

"Yes, you will as soon as you poke your nose in. Try it."

The sounds of "hee, hee, hee's" rippled into Keisha's pointy ears. She looked for the source of the sound while she asked, "Just poke my nose in?"

Keisha didn't like being teased, and her feelings were getting a bit hurt after this long day of being reprimanded by a rabbit. *I think I'll just go back home and ask for a tummy rub.*

"Pleezzz. Just try it."

Keisha cocked her head from side to side. "This hole is only a little bigger than my muzzle."

"Just try." Mitzie's pleading eyes were now close enough to look directly into Keisha's. "Please."

Keisha grumbled, "Silly rabbit is probably just tired from all this work."

Keisha was almost ready to excuse the stupidity of this creature, until she heard some giggles deep within the hole. This sparked her curiosity. She poked her nose inside the hole trying to smell who was giggling.

Bunches of rabbits. I'll bet my cookies on it, she thought as the tip of her black nose slipped into the tunnel entrance.

6. Poof

Poof! In an instant, a dizzy and bewildered dog was standing alone beneath an arched entrance to a cave. "What? Where? Waa, waa, where did this come from?"

As Keisha's eyes traced the rim of the cave entrance, giggles filled the cavern darkness. "Who's in here? Where am I?"

A huge rabbit, at least two times bigger than herself, hopped into Keisha's view and sat on its haunches with its front feet folded across its chest.

"What the heck?" Keisha almost tumbled over backward.

"Don't be frightened, Keisha. It's me."

The voice sounds familiar—only a lot louder. "Mitzie? How did you get sooooo big?"

"I'm not bigger, Keisha. You're smaller."

"Ya. Right." Keisha looked down at her chest and then around at her sides and feet. "I look the same."

However, during her self-examination, she noticed that the trees just outside the cave towered ever so much farther above her head than seconds before. Also, each maple leaf, maybe eight-inches wide, was now big enough for her to lay down on with room to spare. "Everything is so big. What happened?"

She also noticed that the small breeze that had previously just rustled her hair now felt like gusts of wind that could blow her around like the dried leaves whirling around on the forest floor. She braced her legs fearing she might be pushed over or worse, be carried away.

"I don't understand what is happening." Keisha was frightened, but at the same time, doggie curiosity pulled her a little deeper into the cave. While she peered into the darkness, an explosion of multi-colored lights overwhelmed her. Keisha's rear legs went limp, and she slumped onto her rump.

Her eyes, blinded at first, began to adjust to the explosion of colors. She focused on what looked like a fluttering aurora borealis, a shimmering cloud of many colors. To her surprise, they were all about her. Little sparkling humanoid beings were flying all around—giggling, multicolored little people, only slightly smaller than herself. Others were sitting in small ledges of the cave wall; some waving, some lying on their stomachs with chins resting on their hands, all enjoying the spontaneous cabaret.

Keisha was so confused. "I thought fairies were smaller, but you all are just a little smaller than me?"

Mitzie giggled. "Keisha you still do not realize you have been made smaller. Even smaller than me. You are not in a cave, you are walking into my burrow through the tunnel where you poked your nose."

Keisha shook her head. Still in disbelief she muttered, "That cannot be. It just isn't possible. That would make me about six-inches tall." She continued muttering to herself as she followed the huge rabbit down the tunnel.

Crowds of fairies moved back against the wall to allow Keisha enough room to walk down the long corridor. Overwhelmed with curiosity, Keisha followed the huge rabbit even though she didn't know why or where they were going.

She wondered, *Why am I doing this*? Yet, she couldn't help herself. She had to know what was going on.

"Who are these tiny beings?" she asked, as they fluttered all around her.

Excited fairies were flying everywhere. Even after midair collisions they laughed while trying to get a closer look at Keisha. Smiles were on all the cute creatures' faces.

Keisha was the center of attention. If they were not touching her, the fairies were talking to, at, or about her all at once. "Happy to have you here." "Thank you for helping Mitzie." "There she is! There she is!" "Oh isn't she pretty." "What a cute dog." "Her gold eyes are beautiful," and on and on and on and—bump, several more fairies collided, recovered, and giggled with embarrassment.

Within this maze of fairies Keisha continued following Mitzie. She walked through a tunnel that wound downward, and then up; the entire pathway lit by the luminescent beings.

How colorful. It's like a kaleidoscope. I feel like I'm breathing color. Even though she was totally puzzled and a bit fearful, Keisha was exhilarated.

These must be the fairies Carolyn is always looking for. They are here after all. How pretty. I didn't know they twinkled. How do they do that?

Her thoughts were interrupted when an orange-clad fairy darted over her head.

A voice halted her walk. "Welcome, Lady Keisha." A red-clad fairy hovered inches above Keisha's nose. "Will you stay for the party?"

Before Keisha could think of a reply, a dusty blue-clad fairy performed a hovering curtsy. Her long, blond tresses brushed over Keisha's eyebrows just as a male fairy, wearing a rust-colored tuxedo made of winter maples, bowed over her nose.

A much smaller cherub-like fairy tapped Keisha's left paw trying to get some personal attention. "How nice to see you here. I have been wanting for ever-so-long to play with you."

"Play? With me?" All Keisha could do next was stare at this being. Well, this one is more the size I thought fairies would be. It is standing and only tall enough to peer over my paw.

The cherub was ecstatic that Keisha had talked to her. She flitted away so fast that she bumped into the Tuxedo Fairy, spun several backward summersaults, and was caught by two white rose twins with shimmering gold wings.

The cherub's hysterical laughter was contagious. The cavern filled with harmonious echoes of fairy voices. With everyone laughing, Keisha became so overjoyed she started barking, "Woof, woof."

All the fairies applauded her spontaneous participation. The cavern echoed the new melody of laughter, clapping, and barking.

As the reverberating gaiety quieted to a soothing hum, all the fairies turned toward Keisha and bowed. One bowing Alder Fairy stood just in front of Keisha. "Mitzie needed help, and you tried very hard. We are most happy to have you with us."

Keisha only had time to nod before many more greetings, questions, praises, and waves were directed to her.

It seems like a party, she thought, *and I love parties*. Expressing her excitement, she woofed her high pitch, tongue-trilling, doggie laugh. The fairies joined with cheers and applause.

She had only attended human parties. They were fun, even though many guests brought their dogs because Carolyn said they were welcome, too.

Keisha knew in her heart that Carolyn loved her best, but sharing was always difficult. Guests rubbing her tummy and waving their arms and jumping around in a goofy dance, arms and legs kicking around to music helped. *That part was fun*.

There were no other dogs that Keisha could see in this tunnel; only fairies all about and a huge rabbit, bigger than herself, hopping ahead. The rabbit on occasion would look back and repeat, "Follow me. Follow me."

Keisha's mind was whirling in conflicting thoughts. *That's Mitzie. It has to be. But how did she get so big? She seems at least twice as tall as the goats.*

Keisha suddenly stopped walking causing the troupe of fairies behind her to collide into each other. She did not notice the commotion, deep in thought with a startling realization. *That rabbit is not huge. I AM small. This cavern, like Mitzie tried to tell me, IS the new tunnel Mitzie dug into her burrow.* She looked down and around at herself. "Why, I must really be only about six-inches tall." She spoke aloud more to herself, but noticed several fairies fluttering close by nodded in agreement.

Just poke your nose in the hole. Keisha remembered Mitzie's words while she walked deep in thought.

How could poking my nose into a hole make me small? Magic? She remembered this word 'magic'. Carolyn loves writing and talking about the possibilities of magic.

Was this magic? Was it imagination? Was magic imagination? Was imagination magic? Keisha became very excited, "Wow! 'Woof, Woof."

The fairies scrambled all about; covering their ears. "This dog has a very penetrating bark when she gets excited," commented a purple fairy.

Keisha heard the fairy and remembered overhearing Carolyn explain to friends, "Keisha's bark sounds like an elephant forcing its trumpeting through a pin hole."

"Piercing," friends agreed.

Oh, my, worried Keisha as she witnessed the fairies' reaction. She tried to lower her bark into a mild sounding, "Grrf woof." It was difficult since she was so excited. Even when seeing some fairies put their hands over their ears, she couldn't help herself, and leaped about to the rhythm of her barking. She stopped dancing when she saw fairies fly to the ceiling to get out of the way.

"I'm sorry. I'm sorry. This is so wild! So weird. So wonderful! How did I get so small that I fit through a rabbit tunnel? Is this where you all live? In a rabbit tunnel? No wonder Carolyn and I have never seen you."

Keisha was not asking any one particular fairy. Just anyone who was listening.

Three fairies answered, one after the other.

"We do not live in this rabbit tunnel." "This leads to Mitzie's home." "We live beneath the fairy mound."

"The fairy mound? You mean Carolyn is right? Has she ever seen you?" Keisha tried to muffle her barked excitement over the possibilities.

A green-clad fairy laughed as she tried to answer Keisha's question. "Not with her eyes, but she feels us within her spirit."

Several excited fairies talked at once again. "She will see us one day." "Mitzie's tunnel leads into ours." "You are our guest, so wander about . . . but . . . please, no digging."

Keisha voiced her tongue-trilling laugh. "I promise not to dig anywhere. Besides, my paws are not so big now."

She lifted one of her paws during her explanation, then realized how much smaller the fairies' hands were in comparison. She continued to reassure these tiny beings that she was friendly.

"It would take a long time to dig anything here. And it is all lined with wonderful, white wool. So cozy.

"Carolyn would be happy to know the discarded wool was used by fairies to help a friend stay warm."

As Keisha and the fairies continued their conversation, they entered Mitzie's new burrow. Keisha stopped to look all about, barking her amazement. "It is big enough to hold five large rabbits quite comfortably. One rabbit, a recently "tiny'd" dog, and fairies standing around or floating in the air, fit with room to spare."

She watched a team of fairies flying a basket filled with carrots, grasses, and other rabbit munchies. They flew on through the burrow and down the back tunnel.

30

A blue fairy, seeing Keisha's curiosity, landed gently on the dog's head, and then leaned over to look into Keisha's eyes. Keisha was cross-eyed trying to look upward at this fairy who was providing an explanation.

"It is for the midnight feast."

Keisha always checked out a food basket. She couldn't help herself. She smelled nothing in the first basket that caused her to lose her polite behavior . . . but then a second basket came floating over her head.

Delicious aromas of several delectable cheeses drifted down to her nose, carried on the breeze created by fluttering fairies wings.

"Oh my." Keisha watched the basket continue on down the tunnel leading to where she was told was a great hall under the fairy mound.

"I must be a good girl," Keisha continued to remind herself as her mouth salivated.

The blue fairy giggled as she patted Keisha's head. "You are a very good girl." Then she flew off down the tunnel leading to the fairy mound.

Mitzie was sprawled out in one corner of her cave watching. "Welcome, welcome," she said to everyone entering and, "See you later," to those that passed on through.

"Oh, Mitzie. It is quite lovely," a new voice said.

All heads turned to see two more rabbits enter the burrow.

7. A Hullabaloo

"Mother. Father. I was waiting for you. Isn't it wonderful?"

Before Mother Rabbit could answer, her eyes focused on a dog. She had been about to rub noses with her daughter, and almost flipped over backward trying to reverse her approach.

"Dog! Dog! " she screamed.

Father Rabbit didn't see the dog. Nevertheless, he began thumping the ground with his powerful rear legs, his warning to others to run, and hopefully to frighten the dog away.

A bluebell fairy, clad in her winter-white lace dress, dropped from above, putting her petite body between the frightened parents and Keisha. She held her tiny arms out trying to prevent a fight. She was just as frightened as the rabbits, but held her ground long enough to be joined by a swarm of other fairies standing back to back— all with arms raised. Several more hovered above.

Keisha stood defiant. Her back hairs raised into a ridge of hair from neck to tail. She lowered her head and bared her teeth, prepared to defend herself as she glared at the thumping male rabbit.

Normally rabbits don't frighten me, but I am now smaller than they are, after all, and surrounded by strangers. I must defend my honor as well as my body.

Swarms of fairies came from all directions to support Bluebell and the others. The bottom row of fairies linked arms then held on to the feet of fairies standing on their shoulders. Row upon row of fairies thus formed a fairy, chain-link barrier between the parents and Keisha.

"It is okay. All of you calm down. Calm down." Bluebell used her arms and hands and her calming voice to soothe the obviously guarded rabbit couple, their fretful daughter, and most of all Keisha. "Please," she begged, "I have watched Keisha when she is home and know she is not accustomed to being challenged, especially by rabbits."

Keisha flattened her ears and growled ever so softly, but, in these close quarters, it was surprisingly audible to all, especially the rabbits.

"That is not my problem," shouted Father Rabbit, and he thumped his hind legs faster which only caused Keisha to snarl louder.

Thumps and snarls reverberated throughout the entrance and exit tunnels. Before Mitzie could attempt to calm her parents, even more fairies flew from both tunnels into the burrow. They tried to form an impassable barrier between potential enemies.

34

Many fairies attempted to explain the presence of a dog while at the same time Keisha growled, Mother Rabbit squealed, and Father thumped.

"What's all this hullabaloo? Stop it! Stop it this instant! QUIET!"

Quiet it became.

However small this little being was who had flown in from the back tunnel, her voice commanded attention. Keisha was the only one who didn't know this little being, yet Keisha too became quiet while starring in wonderment at this extraordinary fairy.

"Your majesty. Queen Holly Berry. I am so sorry. My parents did not know Keisha had been invited."

Mitzie did the best a rabbit could do to perform a curtsy while trying to explain the situation. Her nose was so close to the ground her voice sounded muffled.

"What? What? Speak up child! I can't understand you." Queen Holly Berry fluttered closer to Mitzie and hovered in the air.

Mitzie was afraid to rise, not accustomed to being in the Queen's presence, nor the focus of her attention. She mustered her courage and raised her eyes, just enough, to meet the Queen's regal gaze. Quickly, she lost her nerve and closed them tight.

"Rise, Mitzie. You are not in trouble . . . although this could be a first." Queen Holly Berry could not help a tiny jest and a smirk. She always remembered Mitzie as a mischievous baby bunny who had nibbled a bit too much from the royal garden on several occasions.

Mitzie rose, but she kept bowing her head, and peeking up as she spoke.

"I'm sorry, Your Majesty. My parents were not told that Keisha would be here. We were all so busy repairing the cave-in we didn't think to tell them."

Mother Rabbit squealed, "CAVE-IN! Oh, my darling. Are you hurt? How did that happen? Your burrow was built so well. Oh, my."

35

The mother's fretful lament could be heard even through the thick wall of fairies who tightened their grip to hold back the push of young rabbits now trying to enter the burrow.

Mitzie and the others on the far side of the fairy-wall could not see that Mitzie's mother and father were joined by her four brothers and six sisters—all yelling questions or demanding to know what was going on.

"Dog? What dog?"

"A dog? In here?"

"Growling?"

"Is Mitzie hurt?"

"Why won't these fairies get out of our way?"

Father Rabbit did his best to calm his children so he could get some answers himself—to no avail. Ten rabbit siblings ran in and out of the tunnel, falling headlong into and over each other, and into the fluttering wall blocking their path. Their frantic voices collided, too.

"Mitzie is in there with a dog?"

"How did a dog get in here?"

"Cave-in?"

"Get out of my way."

The frantic rabbits started digging under the fairy-wall, all voicing a single concern. "We have to dig our sister out from under a cave-in. Or worse, pull her from the jaws of a dog."

The commotion packed the burrow beyond capacity with the rumpus of rabbit squeals, fairy voices, Keisha's growls, the crush of fairy bodies, angry rabbits, and leaping bunnies.

"Stop this instant! Everyone, stand where you are, and STOP THIS RACKET! I can't settle anything if you continue this clamor."

Queen Holly Berry emphasized her command by raising her twisted holly branch staff and then hammering it to the ground. Red holly berry shaped rubies and holly

36

leaf shaped emeralds jingled a sparking melody to an otherwise searing demand for silence.

Though Keisha didn't know her, she sensed this queen had the same commanding presence of her Carolyn. Keisha instantly stopped grimacing and growling, and sat on her haunches, eyes focused only on this three-inch tall, emerald green-gowned queen.

"Murrelda. Round Bottom," the queen said. "Mitzie is with me, and she is fine. No one is buried. No one is hurt. The dog is my guest, my reward to her for helping Mitzie repair her home."

Mother Rabbit was confused. "What happened? Her burrow was fine yesterday. Smartly sound, if I do say so."

All of a sudden, Father Rabbit realized the queen had used his childhood nickname. His pink nose blushed rose red. An especially old grievance raced through his mind. *Will she ever call me by my adult name? And in front of everyone.*

Father Rabbit's embarrassment had a stilling effect on his rising temper—even as he listened to muffled snickers. He flashed a stern fatherly eye toward one of his sons who had joined in the joke.

Everyone knew why the queen called him "Round Bottom." He could never sit upright on his haunches like other rabbits. If he tried, he would roll over onto his back. He had to hunch over when he sat. His mother had assured him that he would grow out of it, but round his bottom remained.

"What happened?" he repeated in a calmer voice. His nose still betrayed his embarrassment.

"Yes. Yes. Were you in the burrow when it caved in, my darling?" The troubled mother needed to see her daughter, but could only beg a question.

"No, Mother. I was coming out to stop Keisha from digging up my tunnel. It was after I bit her on the nose, and she rose up trying to back out causing the branch and earth ceiling to fall in. I was almost outside when it happened."

All Mother Rabbit heard was the "almost," but Father Rabbit's attention remained focused on a nasty dog.

"You have a dog in there that dug up your home? You nipped it on its nose? Good girl! And she is a guest of the Queen? This is totally unacceptable. Just unacceptable."

If there had been room, Round Bottom would have been leaping all around. His frustration was almost too much for a rabbit to handle. He needed to run, hop, jump, leap, and squeal. Those who were pressed close to his body felt his muscles twitch and saw his fur stand on end. All he could do was spin around in a tight circle.

Most of the fairies giggled as they watched Round Bottom, ah, Fleet Foot, hop wildly in his contained spin. They laughed out loud when suddenly Fleet Foot leaped into the air, only to bump his head on the wool covered earthen ceiling. His head broke through a section of the felt. He was doubly rewarded with a painful bump on the head and a shower of dirt.

While trying to clean his face and get irritating particles out of his eyes, he kept complaining. "Why in all the deity's names would you have that miserable mutt invited to our Christmas party? Ahhhh-choooo." Dust had gone up his nose.

"Miserable mutt? Stupid Rabbit!" Keisha made mumbled comments, but didn't move a muscle to reveal her irritation at Round Bottom's rude remarks.

"And how did it get in?" Murrelda was peering all about. "Mitzie, is there a hole in your tunnel that will allow other predators to get in?

"Let me pass! I want to see my daughter!" Murrelda gave a mother's command as she lunged at the fairy barrier.

On the other side of the linked fairies, the queen saw the fluttering wall bulge towards her. "Please calm yourself Murrelda. If you all promise to listen to the whole story, I will let you pass."

"Yes, Yes. We promise. Just please let us through."

Murrelda always kept her promises, but now whispered a worry. "I'm promising not only for myself, but for my family."

She glanced at her anxious children who were still in digging position—yet motionless. "Oh dear, My Queen, I fear my bunnies will not be able to contain their nervous hopping, even if they promise to listen.

"Oh," she moaned, "and in stressful situations Fleet Foot's temper always causes him to act contrary to his promises."

One look at her husband's furry, dirt dusted face and Murrelda recognized stress when she saw it. "What to do? What to do?" Murrelda spun around in frustration.

"RRRRRound Bottom! I did not hear a promise from you." The Queen always rolled her R's when demanding attention from this particular father rabbit. He had been a prankster in his youth, and his tendency to be quick-tempered was well-known.

"RRRRRound BotTOM?" Her tone rose to a high pitch on the 'tom.'

"Yes, Your Majesty. I promise.

"If only to have you stop calling me Round Bottom," he added under his breath. Fleet Foot's head was bowed down in mock humility, to hide his red nose, and to conceal the look of anger in his eyes.

"I'll listen. And then I'll thump that dog's face right out of this burrow . . . mumble, mumble, mumble, mumble.

"Oh, Good Earth," he muttered, "that could cause a cave-in all over again. And, on the other side of this blasted wall of butt-in-ski fairies, sits a dog. I cannot understand how it got in here in the first place . . . grumble, grumble, grumble."

"I will make you keep your promise RRRRrrrrround Bottom. You know I can." The Queen pointed her finger with such determination, its force penetrated the wall.

Fleet Foot felt an actual poke in his nose, which he had to rub with his paw. "Yes, Your Majesty."

He lowered his flushed, red face, muttering, "Will she never forget the time I hopped all over the banquet table? I was a young bunny. Okay, I knocked all the filled cups, dishes, mugs, and goblets on the floor. The Queen made me stay long after the party ended to help clean up the mess as well as all the other party clutter that just happens. Can she never forget? It happened so long ago.

"How can she reprimand a father rabbit so? And in front of my family? I am so humiliated and my family is watching."

Just as quickly, he reminded himself: Queen Holly Berry is a good, kindhearted queen, yet one who demands truthfulness and good behavior.

This made him worry again. "My temper always gets me in trouble," he said aloud.

The queen heard him, nodded and smiled.

8. The Queen's Bidding

"Let them pass my darlings."

The queen waved her arms, and the fairies parted to flutter just above the gathering, ready to do the queen's bidding at a moment's notice—or less.

At once, Murrelda searched for her daughter. When she saw Mitzie among a throng of fairies, she hopped over as fast as she could and began smelling and inspecting every inch of her daughter for signs of injury.

"I'm fine, Mother. Stop worrying. My den is repaired, and I was never hurt."

With her left paw, Keisha brushed her nose which was still showing signs of two well-placed nips. "Like this didn't hurt," she whispered to herself.

Fleet Foot searched for the mutt. His head moved rabbit-quick, left and right, with his eyes scanning the space above the fairies. "Where is it? Where is it?"

"I'm here, sir." Fearing the queen's attention, Keisha had not stood up.

She also, in a most peculiar way, felt somewhat safe surrounded by fluttering fairy wings. The obviously angry father rabbit was bigger than she and very muscular. Keisha knew a thump from one of his powerful hind legs would propel her into the newly dug, burrow walls.

Fleet Foot looked toward the sound of the meek canine yips, only to see a skuzzy, red-haired dog no bigger than a baby rabbit, toes to tip of ears. His intent had been to thump this dog to oblivion, but he couldn't help himself; he broke out in thunderous rabbit laughter. This of course was contagious, and the ripple of laughter and giggles flowed throughout the burrow and beyond into the mound.

Keisha certainly didn't like anyone laughing at her. *Never have, never will*, she thought before defending herself. "I can't help my size, and I don't understand it myself, but I'm still a proud and noble dog who deserves respect. I'm not to be laughed at by a rabbit and a fluttering ceiling."

As Keisha stood up, so did the hackles on her back. Ever so slowly, like a cat stalking a mouse, Keisha advanced on the still chuckling rabbit.

Father Rabbit, distracted by his own amusing thoughts, was no longer taking notice. "I can't believe I was worried. That is a puny, good-for-nothing dog. Hee, hee, hee."

"Gurr rough grerr rup. Stop laughing at me you stupid rabbit."

"Stupid? Ha, ha, ha." Fleet Foot was still smirking as he took his time looking down on this so-called dog. "And tell me silly, LITTLE dog. How were you able to tear apart my bunny girl's home in such a short time? You are barely bigger than a guinea pig."

42

"I was bigger then." Keisha stopped stalking, and tried to stretch her body posture to reflect the size of her pride.

"You were bigger? How did you get so small then LITTLE dog?"

"I don't know. One minute I was apologizing to Mitzie . . . who was telling me to come in . . . and I was telling her I wouldn't fit . . . and as I peeked in the new hole . . . I was suddenly in a cavern." Keisha even forgot about the angry father rabbit. Her thoughts returned to this bewildering situation.

Queen Holly Berry stepped in between the adversaries, arms up, palms forward, turning first to Keisha, and then to Fleet Foot. "I granted our little Mitzie a wish. She wanted to thank Keisha for helping rebuild her home. It is difficult for Mitzie to forgive Keisha. She has good reason to resent dogs in general. To work side by side with one was more than a bit frightening."

Queen Holly Berry turned her attention to Keisha with a wary eye to Fleet Foot. "It is equally difficult for our Lady Keisha to build something, especially for creatures she always chases out of her yard. Keisha has only been a 'pull-a-part-ter' and a digger. She had to learn patience to put sticks into a tightly organized pile instead of pulling them out at random. She had to deliberately help refill a hole rather than obsessively dig one."

All the fairies nodded and chattered in agreement with their queen as she spoke.

"Keisha worked with Mitzie until Carolyn called her for dinner. Keisha is a faithful companion, and had to leave when Carolyn called. Yet, after Carolyn fell asleep, Keisha returned, as she promised, to help finish the burrow. She kept her word." The Queen smiled at the dog.

"We heard Mitzie's cry when this dog dug into her home. We rushed in, prepared to help her. However, as we watched from the cover of trees and brush, Keisha had stopped her digging and offered to help repair the damage. We were watching all the while as Keisha and Mitzie worked together as a team.

"Keisha didn't know until now that, after she had gone home, we finished the burrow. We also raked the woodland and scattered leaves over the exposed dirt to prevent predators from discovering Mitzie's new tunnel."

The Queen returned her attention to Keisha. "We saw the surprise on your darling red-whiskered face. It was delightful to see how you appreciated the appearance of the Fairy Glen. You hadn't realized what your compulsive behavior did with all your digging."

Keisha lowered her head a bit. Although no one saw her blush, blush she did indeed.

Queen Holly Berry did not wish to embarrass her guest, and turned toward Mitzie. "Witnessing Keisha's hard work, and her appreciation for the Glen's beauty, I made a decision. First, I asked Elm Dust to whisper to Mitzie to coax Keisha into the hole. I had previously cast a spell on the new tunnel entrance so that anyone who even poked a toenail into it would become instantly smaller than Mitzie and not be a threat.

"It's a grand idea for all our entrances, just in case. Do you not agree Roun . . . ah, Mr. Fleet Foot?"

She had only turned her head slightly so that her eyes cast a sideways glance at Father Rabbit to make sure he was paying attention.

"My, my ye . . . es, yeess, yes." Fleet Foot was caught by surprise, and could barely stutter an affirmative. "I would be partial to such a spell placed on all our tunnels, Your Majesty." Of course, he did his rabbit best to bow humbly to The Queen.

"Consider it a Christmas present to all, Mr. Fleet Foot."

With that pronouncement, the Queen waved her right arm up and then down as she returned a curtsy to Father Rabbit. Everyone saw the mist of a spell waft from the cavern and swirl on the breeze that carried it throughout the glen. "This spell will settle on all of Seud Araidh, including Huckleberry Field, the Fairy Glen, and the Enchanted Forest."

Keisha knew Carolyn called the back acreage The Enchanted Forest, even though it had too few trees to be called a forest. Yet, Keisha thought, *as enchanted as Carolyn wishes it was, enchanted it is, truly.*

Keisha understood too, that Carolyn's hope for a glen full of fairies was true. And the mound was exactly as those of the Tuatha De Danaan of Ireland: a hollow hill lived in by the Sidhe, the fairies of the mounds.

Who would have believed such wonder exists, and in our woods?

Keisha's defensive attitude melted into a feeling of kinship with these extraordinary inhabitants. *Even in canine mythology, this was told to be true, and now I see it with my own eyes.*

9. Christmas Blessings

"Come!" commanded The Queen.

"All is well. Let us go to the great hall for the Christmas blessing, and share in our bounty of friends, food, drink, music, singing, dancing, and PRESENTS."

"Presents."

"Presents."

"Presents."

The word passed from one fairy to another, pulsating throughout the hall as if the word was a round in a Bardic song—and thus, as fairies always do, they sang it and it became one.

"Presents, presents. Huzzah! Hurray!
The sun shall bring forth Christmas Day.
Rabbits, faeries, and a dog hafe made amends
Our party be graced by fay and friends.
Merriment, wonderment, and the presents,
All to make our celebration most eloquent."

All was forgiven among the adversaries. Father and Mother Rabbit thanked Keisha for rebuilding Mitzie's burrow, and they walked together as friends down the tunnel leading to the Grand Hall deep beneath the mound. As they rounded a bend, brilliant lights momentarily blinded everyone.

Once Keisha's eyes became accustomed to hundreds of flickering candle lights, she stood transfixed. She was at the top of a polished marble staircase looking down fifty stairs into a huge hall decorated in wondrous Christmas grandeur.

To the left, stood several oak tables prepared for a holiday feast. Upon the tables sat polished brass plates and goblets, gold and silver candelabras reflecting candle light off dangling cut crystals, intricately carved drinking mugs and bowls, and huge platters filled with a most delectable banquet.

"Oh! That smells so good." Keisha stood hypnotized by the sights, sounds, and smells.

Fairy musicians were sitting among the branches of the biggest, most beautiful Christmas tree she had ever seen. Keisha recognized the Celtic tune they were playing.

Keisha began talking to any fairy who passed by. "I heard the musicians at the Renaissance Fair play the same song. Carolyn and I often act with them. She is a fantasy actor pretending to be Sahaja, the Apple Tree Fairy. Shugyr and Duende are dressed as unicorns, and I am Chienne Noble De Service. That's French you know. It means Royal Service Dog." Keisha woofed a doggy giggle.

48

"I love riding in the chariot. It is all decorated. Carolyn tries to make it look like an apple tree on wheels."

Fairies listening to Keisha reminisce, giggled. Not to be impolite. They knew something that neither Keisha nor most of the Renaissance Actors did.

One fairy in a group hovering close by spoke to Keisha. "We know about everything you are saying because we are always at the fair. Only a few human friends see us and only some of the animals."

This new information excited Keisha. She barked, "Really. Oh my. That is wonderful to know. Do you remember us?"

"Absolutely. We especially enjoyed Sahaja's encampment and chariot. We played in the tent and flew next to Duende as he pulled you both in the chariot. He didn't know it, but we often rode on his back as you toured the gaily decorated fairground.

"Shugyr was not yet trained to pull the chariot so she stayed at the encampment. But she was never lonely. I think every child in attendance petted her. Many of us hovered close by to ensure her safety.

"No one ever saw us, but after today at least you will. Maybe someday everyone at the fair will see us. That would be so wonderful."

Keisha and the fairies nodded their agreement.

Keisha turned from the group of fairies and was transfixed as she watched the Christmas tree rotate upon a marble platform at the far right end of the hall. She realized the decorations and lights were actually the musicians themselves, but the more she watched them the more amazed she became with the beauty.

Most surprising was their music. She could actually see their music as it flowed from each musician's instrument blending with all the others to make a beautiful melody. She was fascinated watching the melody and the fairies' lights flow together like a crystalline river from the tree, then throughout the hall.

The melodious, sparkling river was whirling and twirling just like the joyous fairies. Some were dancing upon the gold tiled floor and others in the air.

Dancing and music always delighted Keisha, but she had never seen anything like this. She became so excited she couldn't stand still, and ran down the stairs barking all the way.

Fairies shared her excitement by clapping, laughing, and shouting, "Hazzah" as their new canine friend participated in the dance.

Later, Keisha attended the banquet. Of course, she helped eat the cheese from that big basket she saw carried earlier through Mitzie's burrow.

Several fairies chose delectable pieces, and placed them on a brass plate before their canine guest. As quickly as they put a piece of cheese on her plate, it vanished into Keisha's mouth. "My goodness. Our friend really likes cheese."

Watching the dog made the fairies giggle and giggle. Then realizing they may have offended their new friend they apologized.

"It's okay," Keisha assured them. "I just can't help myself, it all taste so yummy."

Keisha also liked presents as much as the fairies. She didn't expect one, as she watched the gifts being passed out, and enjoyed observing joyful fairies opening theirs. She was only a little disappointed when the last one under the tree was given out to a very anxious bunny, Mitzie's brother, Willy.

Willy, put a canine smile on Keisha's face, and chuckles in her belly. Willy was so excited when he got a present he forgot to open it. For some time, he leaped all over the dance floor to the delight of his brothers and sisters and many laughing fairies.

"Keisha. Come forth!"

Keisha was startled to see that she was being addressed again by Queen Holly Berry. "Yes, Your Majesty."

"We have chosen gifts for you, too."

Keisha thought her heart had jumped into her throat as she looked under the tree, her short little tail wagging. She was sure nothing was left, but couldn't help hoping.

The Queen saw Keisha's searching eyes. "My friend, they are not in a package. They are magical gates into the unseen realm of the faeries—one into the Enchanted

Forest, and one into our Glen. Only you may pass through them. They will keep all the other animals out."

"Even the goats, Kindle and Hanna?" Keisha knew Carolyn never wanted the goats in the Fairy Glen.

"Most especially the goats. They eat everything without giving it a thought. My flowers are eaten right down to the nubbins. But, the llama, Duende, and the horse, Shugyr, are much more respectful and sensible."

"My Carolyn says the same thing, Your Majesty."

Queen Holly Berry smiled until she saw a worried expression on Keisha's face. "I know what you are worried about, my darling. You never want to leave Carolyn alone. We admire your loyalty, and you are not to worry. When you visit us, the Guardian Fairies of the Glen will look after Carolyn. She will always be safe while you are gone.

"Carolyn really does want you to play more often, but if she needs you, the Guardians will make sure you are with her instantly."

"Instantly?" Keisha was puzzled by the word "instantly."

"You know . . . Poof!" Queen Holly Berry made a grand gesture with her arms while laughing—in a queenly manner, of course.

Keisha's face mirrored her delight. "Oh . . . How wonderful. This is a wonderful present. Thank you, Your Majesty."

Keisha performed her best, but still awkward, bow. She knew she was going to have to practice this newly learned maneuver to show her respect.

"You are most welcome." The Queen bowed her head to Keisha.

Mitzie timidly hopped to the Queen and tugged lightly on her robe.

"Yes, Mitzie. What can I do for you?"

Mitzie gestured for the Queen to stoop down. She needed to whisper a request. "Your Magesty, if I might ask for one more present. It would help Keisha feel so much better and also make me happy."

"I know. You would like me to heal your new friend's nose." The Queen stood up and pointed her staff towards Keisha.

Keisha, startled by the sudden gesture, worried she might have done something wrong. Less than a second later she felt a tingling on the tip of her nose and the two rabbit nips disappear. "Wow. That is truly magical. My nose feels all better. Thank you, Your Majesty."

"Thank Mitzie for making the request. She wants you to be her friend."

"Thank you so much, Mitzie. That was truly nice of you." She walked to her friend and they rubbed noses.

Then Queen Holly Berry turned gracefully to address everyone. "Now, let us dance and be merry until the sun shines on Christmas day."

"Huzzah. Hurray. " Cheers filled the air until music and laughter took their place.

10. *Full Tummies*

Minutes before the sun peeked over the Cascade Mountains, Keisha left for home. Upon leaving the rabbit tunnel she "poofed" to normal size as the Queen had promised. The fairies helped widen the sliding back door so Keisha could tiptoe in the bedroom and jump lightly to her comfortable corner of the bed.

"Gerrr, ruff. Err ovf. I should have known Mischief Kitty would be here."

"Meow, mow. Hissss . . . erro . . . eroww? Well, well. Where were you all night?" Mischief was very curious. She kept one cat eye on Keisha as she moved just enough to make room for "*that dog.*"

"Geerrrrrr . . . errrr. Wouldn't you like to know?" Keisha's turned around and around before plopping down on the soft mattress, her back to the cat so she wouldn't be annoyed by Mischief's stare.

Carolyn, half awake, felt the bed jiggle and the familiar presence of her beloved companion. She reached out and gently stroked Keisha's head. "Merry Christmas, Sweetheart."

"Meow, meow, meow. Me too, me too, me too." Mischief felt left out of the Christmas greeting.

Carolyn reached over Keisha to pet the complaining cat. "I'm sorry my little Mischief. Do you feel left out? Well, a very Merry Christmas to you, too."

Mischief purred, pleased with the caresses which also took attention away from "that dog."

Keisha understood Carolyn's love for the cat, but she finally couldn't stand it any longer and scooted closer to Carolyn to enjoy some more caresses. Relaxed and happy, she began to drift into slumber and the memory of her wondrous Christmas Eve.

Who would have thought digging a hole would lead to being invited to a wondrous Christmas party with fairies. And I'm invited to return anytime through my magical gates. As long as I promise to dig only in designated areas. Her mouth curved into a canine smile as she slumbered.

Carolyn looked at her sleeping dog. "Why are you so tired little girl? I want to stay in bed awhile longer too, but I have to get up and feed the starving critters their Christmas breakfast."

Keisha growled her discontent, but opened her eyes to watch the morning ritual— Carolyn getting dressed and then searching for her shoes. "Ruff gerr, ruff. I'm sure glad dogs don't wear shoes."

"Ah, here's one." Carolyn got down on her knees to search for the other.

Several passes under the bed, in the closet, and under the two night tables revealed no shoe. It finally was found, after several house-wide and two porch searches, under a towel in the bathroom.

54

Carolyn sighed a "Finally," as did Keisha.

"Let's go feed, girl."

Keisha groaned, but jumped down from the bed and followed Carolyn outside. Full tummy or not, she was driven by loyalty and a reward.

Mischief ignored the activity and curled up on the pillow to sleep a little longer. *When Carolyn comes in from feeding those guys outside I'll come to the kitchen for my treat.*

Soon, Shugyr, Duende, Kindle, and Hanna were eating their oats and hay in stalls covered with fresh straw bedding. They also had apples and carrots as Christmas presents.

Keisha and Carolyn returned to the house for their breakfast . . . oatmeal and coffee for Carolyn, and a doggie cookie on top of a large slice of cheddar cheese for Keisha. The cheese was a special Christmas breakfast treat.

"Woof, woof, ruff ruff err-ruff. Full tummy or not, I always have room for a cookie . . . and any leftover oatmeal."

After her usual quick-sniff inspection, Keisha worried she might be too full to eat any more. But, not wanting to hurt Carolyn's feelings and being a chow hound after all, Keisha made short order of the cookie and then carried her cheese into the living room to enjoy by the warm woodstove.

Mischief was sitting high on Carolyn's flat file, her spot for being feed safe from Keisha perhaps sneaking a bit of cat food. This morning, in addition to some dry cat chow, Carolyn opened a can of tuna and scooped out the contents onto Mischief's dish. "You don't get this everyday little one. I know you like it, so enjoy."

Mischief was already gobbling up the savory fish as Carolyn picked up her mug of coffee and dish of oatmeal and walked to her bedroom. Breakfast in bed was a regular thing to do, but somehow on Christmas morning she felt it was particularly special.

Keisha followed and jumped onto the bed. She snuggled close to Carolyn to make sure she got the last bit of oatmeal. Then she rolled over for more tummy rubs.

"My goodness, Keisha, your tummy is so full. Did I put too much food in your dish last night my little chow hound?"

Keisha 'gerrred,' contentedly. *No. It was fairy cheese and my special Christmas breakfast from you. It was all delicious, and so is this tummy rub.*

"And how's your nose, little girl?" Carolyn leaned closer to Keisha to look.

Keisha tucked her nose under one paw, and closed her eyes. *I can't let her see the injury has disappeared so soon.*

"That's okay. I don't need to touch it. I just want to see if I need to put some ointment on it." She gently lifted Keisha's head to inspect the injury.

Oh dear, worried Keisha. *What can I do? Well too late now. She has a hold of my head.*

Carolyn stared at the end of Keish's nose, turned Keisha's head left and right, twice. "I was sure your nose was nicked last night." She adjusted her glasses, that always slipped down her nose, thinking it would help see better, but still she could not see what she was sure she saw yesterday. She turned her dog's head left and right again and then up and down. "I'm sure you had a cut. Either I was seeing something that was not there or it healed." She laughed, "Ha, ha, ha. Like magic, hey my doggess?"

Keisha looked away as she pulled from Carolyn's hands. *Oh, if she only knew. Magic it was.*

Mischief was at the bedroom door and overhead what Carolyn said and watched the reaction of the dog. "Yeow, eow. Magic, eh? I'll keep my eye on you little dog. Something is going on and I want to know what it is." She jumped up to the foot of the bed to lay down.

Keisha ignored the scowl on Mischef's face and especially gave no response to what she had said. She cuddled closer to Carolyn and licked her hand.

"Well, anyway, you are okay." Carolyn snuggled into her pillow then petted her dog for a little while longer before drifting back into slumber. Her hand relaxed and slipped down to the comforter.

Soon, Keisha nodded off as well for a Christmas morning nap. And so did the entire fairy troupe in the glen who were exhausted from their wild Christmas party that lasted into the wee hours of morning.

Merry Christmas to All
and
To All A Good Nap

www.ingramcontent.com/pod-product-compliance
Lightning Source LLC
Chambersburg PA
CBHW042010080426
42734CB00002B/34